BOEING
747-400

BOEING 747-400

ROBBIE SHAW

EDITOR'S NOTE

To make the Osprey Civil Aircraft series as authoritative as possible, the editor would be interested in hearing from any individual who may have relevant information relating to the aircraft/operators featured in this, or any other, volume published by Osprey Aviation. Similarly, comments on the editorial content of this book would also be most welcome. Please write to Tony Holmes at 10 Prospect Road, Sevenoaks, Kent, TN13 3UA, Great Britain.

ACKNOWLEDGEMENTS

I would like to thank my friends Steve Anisman, Keith Brooks, Matthew Martin and Tom Singfield for their assistance with this project, to Richard Thompson at Kodak UK, and to editor Tony Holmes for his faith in me despite the usual unrealistic timescale he set me! Once again, thanks are due to my wife Eileen for putting up with my enforced absences from time to time, either in the study or in a far-flung corner of the world with a heavy camera bag over my shoulder. I must not forget her proof-reading, a task she relishes! Unfortunately, the Boeing PR department refused my requests to visit Everett and Boeing Field. Perhaps a UK-based photographer just isn't important enough. Readers will notice that a great many of the photographs in this book were taken at Kai Tak, Hong Kong's old airport. I make no apologies for this as, it is one of my all-time favourite photographic locations. During Kai Tak's last six months of operations I made four short visits totalling 17 days, unfortunately the gods were against me, as on each occasion the weather conditions were awful, and I managed just two hours sunshine in all those visits! Unless otherwise credited all photographs are taken by the author.

FRONT COVER *In the autumn of 1994 amidst great secrecy Cathay Pacific unveiled a new livery; however, prior to the event the cat was let out of the bag as some vehicles were delivered to the company complete with the new look. The first aircraft to appear in the scheme was 747-467 VR-HOT, seen here just days after the unveiling*

BACK COVER *747-412F Mega Ark 9V-SFB is seen departing the Alaskan airport. The airline has just one aircraft left to fulfil its order for eight of these freighters*

TITLE PAGE *Four mainwheel bogies each with four wheels are required to distribute the incredible weight of a fully laden 747. The sheer bulk of the Jumbo is evident in this shot of 747-4J6(SCD) B-2460*

RIGHT *Thai Airways International was one of the first members of the Star Alliance which, at its inception, included Air Canada, Lufthansa, SAS, Thai, United and Varig. This alliance will soon be boosted by the inclusion of Air New Zealand, Ansett, All Nippon and Singapore Airlines. The alliance logo now features just behind the cockpit on Thai's 747s, next to the name Chao Phraya in Thai script on aircraft HS-TGM*

First published in Great Britain in 1999 by Osprey Publishing, Elms Court, Chapel Way, Botley, Oxford, OX2 9LP

© 1999 Osprey Publishing Limited

ISBN 1 85532 893 3

Edited by Tony Holmes
Page design the Black Spot
Cutaway drawing on pp126-127 courtesy Mike Badrocke
Origination by Valhaven Ltd, Isleworth, UK
Printed in Hong Kong

99 00 01 02 03   10 9 8 7 6 5 4 3 2 1

Other titles published by Osprey Aviation include:
**THE CONCORDE STORY, BABY BOEINGS,
McDONNELL DOUGLAS JETLINERS,
AIRBUS WIDE-BODIED JETLINERS**
and **TURBOPROP COMMUTERS**

For a catalogue of all titles by Osprey Military, Aviation or Automotive please write to:
The Marketing Manager, Osprey Publishing Limited, P.O. Box 140, Wellingborough, Northants NN8 4ZA, United Kingdom

Or visit our website: http://www.osprey-publishing.co.uk

Contents

An All Nippon standard long range 747-481 with fifteen windows in the upper deck

Introduction

Like its younger cousin the 707, Boeing's model 747 can be said to have significantly changed air travel over the last few decades. These giant jetliners have revolutionised long-haul air travel, and made what was once the preserve of the rich available to many in the developed countries of the world. The Boeing 747 has proved to be *the* long-range airliner and an outstanding success but, without taking away any of the credit from Boeing, that success has also largely been due to a lack of competition from other manufacturers.

Despite its invaluable contribution to civil aviation, the Boeing 747 was actually born from a U.S. Air Force requirement for an ultra long-range transport aircraft. Douglas and Lockheed also submitted their proposals, and it was the latter manufacturer's design, the C-5 Galaxy, which was ultimately chosen.

The 747 design is based on that of the 707 but on a much larger scale. This featured a lower fuselage-mounted swept-wing with four underslung engines and a swept-back tail fin. The cockpit is high on the forward fuselage hump, which, on dedicated freighter variants allows the nose cone to hinge upwards and allow cargo to be loaded directly through the nose. The hump behind the flight deck is also utilised as a passenger area known as the upper deck. This was the first jet airliner to feature double deck passenger compartments, with access to the upper deck via a spiral staircase. In addition to its large passenger capacity of up to 500 passengers, the 747 also has a spacious underfloor hold area for baggage and freight. The amount of cargo which can be carried below decks contributes greatly to the revenue on long haul flights, and it has been said that a 747 on a transatlantic flight can make a profit if the hold is full of freight even if there are no passengers!

The commercial success of the 747 may, in part, be attributed to one man: Juan Trippe, President of Pan American World Airways. It was Pan Am which put the 707 into service, and this distinguished airline pulled off another coup a decade later when it stunned the aviation world on 13th April 1966 by announcing it was to buy 25 747s, soon to be known worldwide as the Jumbo Jet. Despite this massive order, the Boeing Company was rather reticent about formally launching production, as only Japan Air Lines and Lufthansa had so far paid deposits for the type. In July 1966 the company did announce a formal launch of the type, with first deliveries scheduled for 1969. This was a tall order indeed, because, not only were the production facilities at Wichita in

RIGHT *Pan American was the launch customer for the 747, and its fleet of series 100s spent many years traversing the Atlantic Ocean. The airline was also launch customer for the 747SP and, during the 1980s acquired several second-hand series 200s. The aircraft illustrated here is 747-121 N735PA* Clipper Spark of the Ocean, *the tenth Jumbo built. This aircraft will soon celebrate its 29th birthday and is still in service today as a freighter with Polar Air Cargo*

Kansas and Renton in the suburbs of Seattle already working at full capacity, the compact airfield at the latter was unsuitable for this large new aircraft. Therefore before the world's largest airliner could be built, a new site had to be found and constructed – quickly. The place selected was a 780 acre site at Everett, some 30 miles (45 kilometres) north of Seattle. Here, adjacent to the airport at Paine Field, a vast complex was built costing some $200 million. Work on the site began in the late summer of 1966 and by the following year, construction of the first 747 had begun in earnest.

THE FIRST OF MANY

Amazingly, whilst Boeing workers commenced construction of the first 747, much of the new plant was still being built around them. Everett was not, however, solely responsible for the assembly of the Jumbo, other divisions of Boeing throughout the U.S. played their part in the construction of this leviathan. The factory at Wichita produced several components for the nose section, whilst a new plant at Auburn, some 20 miles (32 km) south of Seattle was responsible for manufacturing wing panels. The same factory also built the main wing assembly jig for use at Everett.

Despite the size of the Boeing Company, the 747 would not have flown without the assistance of other U.S. aircraft manufacturers, as well as numerous aerospace component companies in almost every state, who were sub-contracted to produce parts ranging from rivets to main fuselage sections. The larger corporations involved included Fairchild, LTV, Northrop and Rockwell, the latter building the lower centre fuselage sections and wing leading-edges at its Tulsa, Oklahoma plant. In California Northrop produced components for the main fuselage, while Fairchild was responsible for the manufacture of all leading and trailing-edge wing flaps, ailerons and spoilers. LTV's share of the work included the rear fuselage, tailplanes, vertical fin and the rudder: these items combined were considerably larger than the A-7 Corsair II, the last aircraft built by the Dallas company.

In all, some six million parts are required to build one 747, a process which used to take about 21 months. Most of the component installation and sub-assembly work is completed by the time the aircraft begins to take shape on the main production line, and only the final two months of this process are undertaken in the aircraft assembly hall at Everett.

When the aircraft is almost structurally complete it is still unpainted. At this stage the aircraft can now be moved on its own wheels to the fitting out bay, where electric, hydraulic, air conditioning and pressurisation systems are connected. Here, also, myriad items ranging from toilets and galleys to the many signs that appear in a modern airliner are installed. Seats and carpeting are also fitted at this stage, although some airlines prefer to fit their own after the jet has been delivered. The same applies to the often complex in-flight entertainment systems which can be fitted in today's jetliners.

ABOVE *Many older series 100s and 200s have been retired from passenger service and converted to freighters. Atlas Air Cargo is one of several American freight carriers who use the type, with former Thai International 747-2D7B example N523MC seen taxying to the cargo ramp at Sharjah in the United Arab Emirates*

As the engines are fitted the cockpit instrumentation and navigation aids are added, and internally the machine is nearing completion. It is now time for the roll-out and, as the hangar doors are opened wide, the bare metal structure slowly emerges under tow by a powerful tug. Although unpainted, the metal appears dull and lifeless this is due to a protective layer of coating applied to prevent corrosion, which will not be removed until the aircraft is in the paint shop and ready to receive its customer's livery.

The 747 is then towed across a specially constructed 60ft (18m) wide bridge over a road to another part of the site which contains the paint shop and flight test area on Paine Field. A handful of systems tests are then completed before the aircraft enters the paint shop, which is fitted with specially controlled heaters to provide optimum drying conditions. A typical 747 will receive on average some 250 gallons (565 litres) of paint, and much masking off of the fuselage and other parts is undertaken whilst the aircraft is in the paint shop in fact, Boeings painters spend more time on preparing a 747 for spraying than they actually do decorating it.

The gleaming new aircraft will then be towed to the pre-delivery and flight test ramp, where it will be parked alongside a dozen or so other aircraft (including 767s and 777s) in varying stages of final preparation. This includes filling the fuel tanks and checking for leaks, and systems checks prior to engine runs. The aircraft will also undergo two precise measuring operations: a compass-swing to finely calibrate the aircraft's navigation equipment; and the accurate weighing of the airframe. The latter is of vital importance because, although each aircraft is constructed and assembled to the same exacting specifications, no two airframes ever weigh the same.

Once the engine runs and other systems checks have been satisfactorily completed, the aircraft will move under its own power for the first time to carry out taxi tests. Then it is time for its maiden flight and any subsequently required test flights. These are flown by both Boeing and customer pilots, and following their successful conclusion the aircraft will be handed over to its proud new owner.

The prototype 747, registration N7470, was rolled out on 1st September 1968 accompanied by great pomp and ceremony; quite rightly so, as this great achievement had been completed a day ahead of the date planned at the start of the programme. The prototype was actually painted prior to the official roll-out ceremony, where it appeared in a red and white colour scheme, adorned with the logos of the 27 airlines that had ordered the type at the time. After a series of high-speed taxi tests had been completed, the aircraft was fitted with additional instrumentation. This took longer than expected, and the aircraft missed its scheduled maiden flight of 17th December, a date chosen to commemorate the 65th anniversary of the Wright brothers first flight. The maiden flight actually took place on 9th February 1969, although it had to be cut short after just one hour following a minor malfunction with the trailing-edge flaps.

THE 747 FAMILY

The certification programme involved the first five aircraft built and required over 1,500 hours of flying in a ten month period, culminating in F.A.A. certification on 30th December 1969. The first production variant of the 747 was the series 100, and the second aircraft built was appropriately registered N747PA and christened *Clipper America* for Pan American. The airline had intended putting the type into service in December 1969, but following Boeing's delays described above, and further niggling engine problems, this was delayed until February 1970. On the 22nd, the inaugural 747 service was flown from New York to London/Heathrow, although this flight was subject to delay due to those engine problems. The powerplant in question was the Pratt & Whitney JT9D-1 which, because of an unexpected increase in weight of the 747 during production , was far from ideal.

Matters improved significantly with the introduction of the more powerful JT9D-3AW with water injection. General Electric CF6 and Rolls-Royce RB211 engines were later certificated for use on the 747. Typical seating capacity on the 747-100 ranged from around 350 in mixed configuration to about 490 in a high-density one-class layout. The maximum capacity was increased to 516 with the introduction of the 747-100SR (Short Range) version built specifically for the Japanese market where All Nippon and Japan Airlines used the type on a number of short one-hour long flights between major cities. Main production of the 100 series was terminated in 1976, although a few for Saudi and a number of SR variants were produced during the early 1980s. In recent years a number of 747-100s have been converted to freighter configuration as newer models have taken their places in passenger service. A total of 207 747-100s have been built, 111 of which were still in service by the beginning of 1999.

Boeing quickly realised that the 747 was capable of further improvement, particularly with the availability of more powerful engines from the three major powerplant manufacturers. The manufacturer also went about strengthening the airframe and landing gear of the aircraft,

thus enabling them to increase significantly the 747's maximum take-off weight, as well as allowing the customer the choice of an increase in payload or fuel. Designated the 747-200, it had the same external dimensions of the 100, but internally the upper deck was increased slightly to increase passenger capacity. Most airlines fitted out the upper deck exclusively for first class passengers, and this trend has continued with subsequent models.

The first 747-200, the 88th Jumbo built, first flew on 12th November 1970, and was delivered to Northwest Orient Airlines as N611US. A higher gross weight variant, the 200B soon became the favoured type for many customers. Other variants include the 200F freighter with an upward hinging nose section which opens to allow cargo to be loaded directly. This variant required a strengthened floor, and both these features were replicated on the 200C Combi variant. The 200C however was not a great success, handicapped by the amount of time required to change from one role to another.

A more popular Combi model was the SCD (Side Cargo Door) variant, with the door in the port rear fuselage. Operators of this type tend to work more or less

LEFT *A little over half of the 45 distinctively shaped 747SP variants remain in service, including two with Syrianair. Both have served continously with the airline since delivery in 1976, with YK-AHA being named 16 November*

RIGHT *The 747-300 variant kicked off the stretched upper deck concept, which resulted in Singapore Airlines dubbing their aircraft BIG TOP. When the airline introduced the 747-400 – which has the same upper deck dimensions as the 300 – a little artistic licence was used with the MEGA TOP title. As increasing numbers of 400s are delivered, Singapore Airlines is slowly disposing of its 300 fleet, though N123KJ is still in use*

permanently in this mixed configuration, with passengers in the forward cabin and freight in the rear. The 200 is also used in the military. The U.S.A.F. operates it as the Presidential Air Force One under the designation VC-25A, while the Airborne Command Post variant is the E-4. The pre-revolutionary Imperial Iranian Air Force used the type both as transports and in-flight refuelling tankers.

To increase capacity further, Boeing's designers came up with the novel idea of increasing the capacity of the upper deck by stretching it rearwards by 23ft (7m). This variant is known as the SUD (Stretched Upper Deck), and K.L.M. had ten of its 200B and 200C models retro-fitted to this standard. Japan Airlines and U.T.A. also had a few aircraft modified to SUD standard.

As the number of 200s in passenger service decreases, many have found a new lease of life as freighters traversing the world's oceans in the colours of the increasing number of cargo airlines. A total of 393

series 200s were built, 364 of which were still in service into 1999.

The next member of the Jumbo family was the 747SP (Special Performance) which was announced in August 1973. Within weeks Boeing had received an order for ten from Pan American. The 747SP is immediately identifiable, for although it has the same wingspan as the previous two models, the fuselage length is reduced by 47ft 1in (14.35m), producing a somewhat stumpy appearance. The tailplanes and fin have been increased in size and height respectively.

The raison d'être of the SP is its long range, although its higher cruising speed and reduced fuel consumption were attributes that made it an ideal aircraft for long, thin routes. Naturally, the passenger capacity was reduced; about 331 in a three-class layout and up to 440 in an all-economy fit. The first SP was the 265th 747 built, and the maiden flight was on Independence Day, 4th July 1975.

resulting increase in weight – some 9,000lb, (4,084.2 kg) – which resulted in the maximum range being reduced by 1,674 miles (2,695 km). This was the main reason why sales of the 300 failed to meet expectations, particularly when compared to the success of the 200B. The first series 300, a Combi for Swissair, flew on 5th October 1982. This was the 570th Jumbo built. Japan Airlines operates several 300s, and in this carrier's service passenger capacity ranges from 329 in a three-class configuration to 563 in the 300(D) domestic variant. Production of the 747-300 ceased in 1990, with the last aircraft being delivered to Sabena. A mere 81 were built, 78 of which are still in service. Two have been lost in service with Korean Air and U.T.A., though the latter's loss was due to a fire while under maintenance at Paris/Charles de Gaulle airport.

Surprisingly, the largest 747 operators have not been the U.S. mega-carriers, but the national airlines of two small and similarly sized island nations. In second place is British Airways, which operates the series 100/-200 and 400. In November 1998 the airline retired its first series 100, the 23rd 747 built, after almost 25 years service. Japan Airlines is the largest 747 operator and it received its 100th Jumbo in November 1998. It currently has 82 of the type in service, including two ageing 100s. Of the major variants, the SP is the only one never to have served with the airline. The national airline of a much smaller island nation, Singapore, holds the distinction of being the third largest 747 operator of all time.

To demonstrate how times have changed, remember that the 747 found a niche and became *the* mode of transport across the Atlantic Ocean. Now however, only the major European carriers operate the Jumbo on transatlantic routes, whilst U.S. carriers use smaller types like the 767, 777 and MD-11. This of course means that those carriers have had to increase the frequency of service. They often then complain that they cannot get additional slots at European airports because of congestion and lack of slots! Wouldn't it be better for all concerned if they reduced frequency and used larger aircraft? I'm sure the environmentalists would agree!

Production of this unique aircraft terminated in August 1982, although one further example was built in 1987 for the United Arab Emirates Government. In fact in recent years the 747SP has proved a popular aircraft in the VIP role for several Middle Eastern governments and rich individuals. Only 45 747SP variants were built and, although none has been lost in accidents, just over half of these remain in service, with the others in storage.

Following on from the Stretched Upper Deck modification on the series 200 the next logical step by Boeing was to offer this feature as standard, thus the 747-300 was born. To maximise capacity in the upper deck a straight staircase replaced the spiral staircase. The Stretched Upper Deck feature has both good and bad points to it. On the positive side, the aerodynamics were improved by the streamlined shape, resulting in a slight increase in airspeed from Mach 0.84 to 0.85. This advantage, however, was more than cancelled out by the

Authors Note - Boeing Designations

For those unfamiliar with Boeing designations featured in this book some explanation is necessary. The manufacturer allocated every customer a two-digit code from 01 to 99, however when those numbers ran out a letter/number combination was used. British Airways for example has the customer code 36, therefore the 747 series 100, -200 and -400 of the airline are designated 747-136, -236 and 436 respectively. Eva Air was a later customer whose designation is 5E, therefore its 747-400s are designated 747-45E.

Chapter One

BOEING 747-400

The latest variant of the 747, the series -400, is currently the world's largest, heaviest and most powerful airliner, and is the only model of the Jumbo now in production. The -400 was developed by Boeing when the company became aware in the 1980s that current models of the 747 were either incapable of flying non-stop on some of the most popular long-haul routes, or could only do so with reduced payloads. These routes included services from Western Europe to Asia and transpacific services to Asia from the U.S. At the time, the economies of many Asian countries were booming, and there was no doubt that there was a demand for such an aircraft.

The formal go-ahead was announced in May 1985, and soon afterwards orders began to pour in. By the time the prototype was rolled out on 26th January 1988, deposits had been received for over 100 aircraft. At first glance the 400 is difficult to distinguish from the series 300, which is not overly surprising as both types share a common fuselage, including the Stretched Upper Deck. However, there the resemblance ends. The wings are structurally re-designed with aluminium-lithium alloy skin panels, thus saving about 6,000lb (2,722 kg) in weight.

The wing span is increased to 211ft 5in (64.44m), and at the end of each wing is the most striking visual feature

RIGHT *Boeing 747-400s in the huge final assembly plant at Everett.* (Boeing Airplane Company)

— a 6ft (1.83m) high winglet which is canted out at an angle of 290°. When the wing is full of fuel however, the outer portions bend downwards, the resulting effect being that the winglets are angled further outwards and increase the wing span to 213ft (64.92m). This increase in span has enabled the manufacturer to add a sixth variable camber leading-edge flap section instead of the five found on other variants. Constructed of graphite composites, the winglets improve the aerodynamics of the wing and help the series -400 to achieve a fuel saving of up to 17% over the earlier series 200, and 13% over the 300.

Boeing's engineers did in fact want an even greater increase in wing span, however the airlines, and especially the airports, were not so keen. Many airports were already struggling for space because of the ever increasing wide-body fleets of many airlines, and a further increase in span would have caused chaos as airports tried to re-design parking stands to fit the latest monster. The -400

offers an increased fuel capacity, including fuel tanks inside the horizontal tail. This increases the design range of the 747-400 to 8,290 miles (13,340 km) against the series -200's 5,290 miles (8,510 km).

The -400 can operate ultra-long range sectors such as London to Hong Kong and Tokyo, and Los Angeles to Auckland and Sydney, typically carrying 418 passengers in a three-class configuration. Maximum capacity is 569, and -400(D) (Domestic) variants operated by All Nippon and Japan Airlines are so configured. These aircraft are structurally reinforced, including the landing gear, to compensate for the significantly higher number of cycles they will fly. They are also identifiable by the lack of winglets, as on the short sectors employed it is more cost effective to operate without them. This of course makes it very difficult to distinguish them from the series 300.

One area in which the 400 differs from other variants that is not immediately apparent is the flight deck. Modern glass cockpit avionics with multi-colour electronic displays reduce cockpit workload by at least a third, and possibly as much as a half according to Boeing. For this reason the flight deck crew comprises two pilots, the flight engineer being dispensed with. With the increased range Boeing have made provision for crew rest areas, with a small space behind the cockpit available for pilots. Cabin crews have a rest area fitted with bunks in the rear of the passenger cabin. As many of the sectors flown are extremely long, many airlines allocate additional crew member(s) to share the workload by working in shifts.

The three main engine manufacturers allow operators to choose from the General Electric CF6-80, the Pratt & Whitney PW4056 and Rolls-Royce RB211-524. When the 400 was first announced, the RB211-524G engine was the most powerful available, producing 56,000lb of thrust. Now the RB211-524H is available, and the company ultimately hopes to offer an RB211 with a thrust of 80,000lb. There is no doubt that the RB211 is currently the most powerful, yet most fuel efficient engine available today, and for this reason RB211 powered 747-400s of British Airways and Qantas have been able to increase their maximum take-off weight to 875,000 lb (396,895 kg). This permits Qantas to carry up to 15 more passengers, or their equivalent weight in cargo, on the ultra long haul 6,500nm (12,050 km) 14 hour 45 minute journey between Los Angeles and Sydney.

Having found that the SCD (Side Cargo Door) Combi variant sold well in earlier models the manufacturer soon made such a variant available for prospective -400 customers, and they have not been disappointed with the response. This variant is known officially by Boeing as the -400(M).

The majority of -400 operators have a seating capacity in the range of 380-450 passengers. The total of

RIGHT *The prototype 747-400 during an early test flight in Boeing colours. At the completion of its flight test work the aircraft was refurbished and handed over to Northwest Airlines as N661US in December 1989 (Boeing Airplane Company)*

course depends very much on the ratio of first, business and economy seats. A typical seat pitch in economy for instance would be 34in, yet in first class this could be as much as 61in. As an example, compare the seating capacity and ratio of first/business/economy seats of 747-400s operated by Japan Airlines and United Airlines. The Japanese carrier seats a total of 304 passengers in a 19/157/128 configuration, whilst United seat 418 in an 18/80/320 configuration, with a greater emphasis on economy and less in business class. I should point out that some carriers, including J.A.L and United, operate their aircraft in several different configurations, with certain aircraft dedicated to specific routes to cater for specific types of traveller.

The maiden flight of the first 747-400, the 696th Jumbo built, took place on 29th April 1988. This aircraft, registered N401PW, was destined for launch customer Northwest Airlines, although it was first put through its paces in order to gain type certification. During this work, at Moses Lake in Washington State, the aircraft entered the record books for the heaviest take-off, at 892,450 lb (404,994 kg), before eventually being handed over to the customer in December 1989 as N661US. The next two aircraft were for Lufthansa and Cathay Pacific, but were first used to certify the type with the CF6-80 and RB211 engines respectively. The honour of the first 747-400 to be delivered to a customer went to Cathay Pacific: VR-HOO was delivered to Hong Kong on 28th August 1988, less than a month after its maiden flight.

A proud moment for Boeing occurred at Everett on 10th September 1993 with the roll-out of the 1,000th 747 (9V-SMU). In front of 18,000 cheering workers, this latest series -400 emerged from the cavernous hangar as executives of Singapore Airlines, the aircraft's owners, looked on. A dedicated freighter variant, the 747-400F is featured later in this book.

By 30 November 1998, 566 747-400s of all variants had been ordered, 453 of which had been delivered, and are currently operated by 37 airlines. Only one aircraft has been lost to date, a remarkable record given the amount of hours the fleet spends in the air every day. The aircraft in question was 747-409 B-165 of China Airlines, which was only a few months old when it crashed on 4 November 1993. Whilst landing on runway 13 at Hong

Kong's Kai Tak airport in heavy rain and strong winds, caused by a nearby typhoon, it soon became apparent to the crew that they were unlikely to be able to stop the aircraft before the end of the runway.

The pilot apparently tried to make the 90° turn onto the taxiway at the end of the runway, but the jet was travelling too fast and gently slid backwards into the murky waters of Victoria Harbour. As a tribute to Boeing engineering, it floated just like an ocean liner, and all 296 passengers and crew escaped to safety.

Afterwards the 747 remained afloat, but its tail fin was an obstruction to any other movements at the now closed airport, and it therefore had to be blown off by explosives so that the airport could re-open again. The 747 was subsequently recovered from the harbour, but due to the damage caused by the explosion and the corrosion caused by its immersion in salt water, it was eventually reduced to scrap in the hangar at Kai Tak.

Boeing has been examining several ways to improve the 747-400, ranging from aerodynamic improvements to new derivatives with both longer and shorter fuselages. There are two proposed versions of the 747-400X. Through increased fuel capacity this model will increase range to over 14,000 km, and be designated the -400ER when launched. It would utilise the strengthened wing of the -400F and be powered either by uprated or new engines. Passenger capacity would be the same as the current -400, but increased fuel capacity will take the Maximum Take-off Weight (MTOW) to 902,380 lb (409,500 kg).

BOTTOM *Despite the large number of 747s which have served with U.S. airlines, only two, Northwest and United, have adopted the -400 passenger variant. This must be rather disappointing for Boeing as, had it not been for the European and Asian customers, the aircraft would have become a great white jumbo. Northwest Airlines was the launch customer with an order for 10 aircraft, the first of which was delivered in January 1989. That aircraft – 747-451 N663US – is seen here at Beijing/Capital airport*

RIGHT & BELOW, RIGHT
*Northwest uses its
747-400 fleet almost
exclusively on transpacific
services, particularly to
Japan. To commemorate its
50th year of those services
N670US has been painted
in a special Worldplane
livery. The Worldplane
scheme features paintings
of scenes representing the
cities served by the airline's
747-400 fleet. On the port
side of the white fuselage
scenes depicted are from
Manila, Singapore, Bangkok,
Hong Kong, New York,
Osaka and Seattle. The
aircraft is at Osaka/Kansai
airport. A close up of the
Bangkok and Hong Kong
scenes is shown right*

The proposed 747-400X stretch would also utilise the wing of the -400F, but a small increase in length would increase capacity by 16% – about 70 passengers. The penalty being a slight reduction in range compared with the current -400. The -400Y is more complex, requiring an increase in both length and wing span to enable an increase in capacity by 90 passengers and a range of almost 14,500 km. This variant requires new engines, with the Rolls-Royce Trent and the GE-PW GP7000 being the likely candidates. Plans for the larger series -500X/-600X were shelved in January 1997.

Some of the decisions taken by Boeing's management in recent years have baffled many in the industry. Several years ago, in a bid to cut costs, the company dispensed with about 20% of its workforce, with Everett, and the more experienced, and therefore costliest workers bearing the brunt. However, very shortly afterwards the manufacturer decided to increase production rates, and found this very difficult to do. In recent years it has been hiring new workers at a phenomenal rate; but the loss of much of the experienced workforce caused serious difficulty. Not only has the company failed to increase production sufficiently to cope with demand, but the quality of work has declined. There are rumours that a number of airlines have voiced their disquiet about the quality of Boeing's work at the moment. Even United Airlines has (allegedly) told Boeing to get its finger out, or it will have no qualms in ordering even more aircraft from arch rival Airbus Industrie. The economic situation which has affected much of Asia during 1998 has now caused

ABOVE *Schemes on the starboard side of Worldplane N670US from the rear forwards include San Francisco, Minneapolis-St. Paul, Los Angeles, Shanghai, Tokyo, Beijing, Seoul, Jakarta and Honolulu*

RIGHT *United Airlines is the largest U.S. 747-400 operator and took delivery of the first example on 30th June 1989. This aircraft, 747-422 N171UA was given the name Spirit of Seattle II. Uniteds 747400 fleet has grown steadily and currently stands at 35 aircraft with a further 16 on order, which will soon take it up there alongside the big boys in the operators league table. Hub of the fleets operations is Los Angeles, where N187UA is seen on final approach*

BELOW *United Airlines current livery was introduced at the end of January 1993, and is seen here on 747-422 N180UA lined up for departure from runway 13 at Kai Tak. The airline has steadily increased services to Hong Kong, including a round the world service on which passengers arriving from the U.S. on the 747 continue westwards on a 767 to Delhi and London, where the circle is completed by 777 services across the Atlantic*

BOTTOM, RIGHT *Heavily laden United 747-422 N196UA climbs off Kai Taks runway 31 bound for Los Angeles, barely clearing the rooftops of apartment blocks in Kowloon*

LEFT *Seen from the checkerboard, United 747-422 N196UA claws its way through the murky conditions on its final approach to Kai Tak's runway 13. Sadly, this incredible view is no longer available, and the many enthusiasts from around the world who travelled to witness such scenes only have photographs or memories to remind them. Unfortunately the new Hong Kong airport at Chek Lap Kok has no observation deck or such facilities. Rumour has it that the airport authority approached the British Airports Authority for advice on the matter, and the reply was don't bother. Perhaps more progressive airports like Frankfurt and Zurich should have been approached instead, for some more sympathetic advice. Following the chaotic scenes since the opening of the new airport, local newspapers have renamed it Chek Lap Kok Up !*

the Boeing management to have another rethink. Although order cancellations have been minimal, the management issued a (to the author) quite amazing announcement in the first week of December 1998. Production is to be drastically reduced. The 747-400 will be reduced from the present 3.5 aircraft a month to two a month in 1999, and thereafter to just one! Even more of a bombshell was the announcement that 48,000 employees would lose their jobs over the next two years. During the 1990s Boeing's workforce has gone up and down like the proverbial yo-yo because of an inability to match production capacity to customer demand. That, more than anything, has been the company's Achilles heel in recent years, and has played into the hands of its only real competitor. Having said this, it must be remembered that no other industry works on such long lead times: and with such phenomenal amounts of capital investment.

RIGHT *The road and rail bridge linking the man-made island on which Kansai airport is located with the nearby mainland, provides an interesting backdrop for United's N178UA. The increasing number of series -400s joining the airline's inventory has allowed it to expand services to Kansai as well as Tokyo*

BELOW RIGHT *Both of Canada's major carriers are 747-400 operators, Canadian Airlines International being the first in December 1990. Three 747-475 aircraft were acquired over the next 17 months. These were joined by a fourth aircraft in April 1995 which had originally been destined for Philippine Airlines, but who could not afford it, and the aircraft spent a short period in store. Photographed under tow to the airline's Vancouver maintenance base is 747-475 fleet number 884, C-FBCA, named GW Grant McConachie*

LEFT *Canadian Airlines International four strong 747-400 fleet is employed solely on transpacific routes out of Vancouver, including Hong Kong, where C-FBCA is seen turning onto final approach. The 747s have replaced DC-10s which used to operate this route*

RIGHT & OPPOSITE, TOP
Air Canada has been operating the Boeing 747 since 1971, and three 747-433(SCD) variants joined the inventory in a three month spell in mid 1991. In contrast to Canadian Airlines International, Air Canada employs its series -400s on transatlantic routes, particularly to London Heathrow. Featuring the carriers old livery, C-GAGN prepares to depart the London airport

BELOW *Displaying Air Canada's current livery of a boring all-white fuselage 747-433(SCD) C-GAGN taxies to the ramp at Toronto whilst in the background an A340 lands on runway 24L*

RIGHT *Varig took delivery of three 747-400s between May 1991 and April 1993. Following financial problems however, the airline returned them in the latter half of 1994, one going to Garuda and two to Air New Zealand, with whom they still serve. One of the latter aircraft, 747-475 PP-VPI is seen on approach to Heathrow. The customer number of this aircraft indicates it was originally destined for Canadian Airlines, but not taken up. Varig has since placed an order for six series -400s, the first of which should be delivered in 1999*

INSET *First European customer for the series -400 was Lufthansa, a strong supporter of Boeing products. Lufthansa's first series -430 was the second -400 built, and the aircraft is named after the capital city, Bonn. The first of this variant actually to be delivered to the airline, D-ABVA Berlin, was however the ninth of the type built. It is seen here about to land on runway 25L at Los Angeles. Two other aircraft inbound to the busy Californian gateway are visible in the background*

RIGHT *In the early 1990s Lufthansa found it was unable to make a profit on services to Australia and decided to give the route to its charter subsidiary Condor Flugdienst. As Condor did not have an adequate aircraft to operate the service, Boeing 747-430(SCD) D-ABTD Hamburg was leased from Lufthansa and operated in full Condor livery between June 1993 and February 1996. The aircraft is seen here passing through Bangkok in March 1995. The aircraft has since returned to the Lufthansa fleet*

OPPOSITE, BELOW *All of Lufthansa's 747-430 fleet are named after German cities, with Munchen (Munich) allocated to D-ABVL, illustrated here with the apartment blocks of Kowloon in the background. The airline's 747-430 fleet currently numbers 22 aircraft, seven of which are SCD models. A further seven 430 pure passenger variants are presently on order*

LEFT *A Lufthansa 747-430 parked at gate B35 at Frankfurt during a turnround. This view graphically demonstrates just how high above the ground the flight deck is*

RIGHT *British Airways is not just the largest 747-400 carrier in Europe, but the largest in the world. The fleet currently stands at 50 aircraft, although two are operated in the markings of British Asia Airways. Outstanding orders number seven aircraft. It had been much higher, but owing to the economic downturn in Asia some of these have been cancelled and additional orders for the smaller Boeing 777 have been placed instead*

LEFT A British Airways Boeing 747-436 about to land on runway 26 at Gatwick. The relative size of the winglets is evident in this shot

BELOW During the winter of 1996/97 a fleet rationalisation saw the 10 Gatwick-based Boeing 747-200s move northwards to Heathrow, with 14 747-400s moving in the opposite direction. Boeing 747-436 G-BNLD City of Belfast taxies at Gatwick with the North Terminal visible in the background

RIGHT *The Shell refuelling bowser looks like a toy compared to the bulk of the 747-400 in this plan view. Note also the size of the large flaps*

OPPOSITE, ABOVE *City of Belfast 747-436 leaves runway 26 at Gatwick. BA's practice of naming its 747-400s after British cities ceased with the introduction of Operation Utopia, the airline's introduction of tail colours from around the world*

OPPOSITE, BELOW *Prior to the unveiling of Operation Utopia colour schemes several 747-436 aircraft were painted in an interim scheme, so that when the time came to unveil Utopia they could receive the full livery very quickly. Formerly City of Southampton, G-BNLG is seen in interim scheme prior to being painted in the Whale Rider scheme*

RIGHT *To portray the sheer bulk of the 747-400 this angle on 436 G-CIVS Whale Rider must be favourite*

BELOW RIGHT *The most powerful engine available to power the 747-400 is the Rolls-Royce RB211-524H2*

ABOVE *Adorning the tail of 747-436 G-CIVM as it approaches Hong Kong is the Japanese design Nami Tsuru, which translates to Waves and Cranes. This scheme now features on three 747-436 aircraft, the others being G-CIVR and VX*

LEFT *There are now over 30 different schemes adorning the tails of British Airways aircraft. The colourful scene on the tail of 747-436 G-BNLN is Nalanji dreaming, an Australian Aborigine design first seen on a Qantas Boeing 747-300. Lima November is seen here on take-off from its Gatwick base as flight BA2075 bound for Lagos*

RIGHT *The colourful African theme Ndebele/Emmly Masanabo is shown to good effect on 747-436 G-BNLO as it makes a smooth landing at Gatwick. Emmly Masanabo has a twin sister Martha, and her scheme also appears on several B.A. aircraft, including a 747-436. Note the spoilers and thrust reversers deployed*

RIGHT *Although Lufthansa was the first European customer for the 747-400, KLM was the first European recipient of the type, a week ahead of the German flag carrier. Like Lufthansa, KLM operates a mixed fleet of pure passenger and SCD variants, with the Combi model being more prevalent. Only five pure passenger 747-406 aircraft are operated, of which PH-BFB Bangkok is one*

BELOW *KLM names its 747-400s after cities served and, apart from two exceptions, the last letter of the registration corresponds to the initial of that city. The aircraft named City of Lima is 747-406 PH-BFL, seen here landing at its Schiphol base*

BELOW *The Side Cargo Door is clearly visible on the port rear fuselage of 747-406(SCD) PH-BFD Dubai during push-back from pier F at Amsterdam/ Schiphol. KLM's Combi fleet numbers 11 aircraft, with the 11th example, PH-BFV Vancouver, delivered in spring 1999. Four of these aircraft operate as KLM Asia*

KLM's long range fleet includes Boeing 747-200, -300 and -400 aircraft, which are supplemented by 767s and MD-11s. Seen on rotation from runway 24 at Schiphol is 747-406(SCD) Melbourne. Although only just airborne, note how much flex there is in the outer wing

INSET *Three sections of leading edge slats deployed help to provide lift during take-off and climb out. The powerplant selected by KLM for its 747-400s is the General Electric CF6-80C2B1F: and some people find aircraft designations confusing!*

MAIN IMAGE *As previously mentioned, KLM has four 747-406(SCD) aircraft operating in KLM Asia titles but, unlike British Airways and Swissair, the Dutch carrier does not feature a separate tail logo. Photographed during a turn round at Osaka/Kansai is PH-BFM Mexico City*

RIGHT *Air France currently operates all four major 747 variants; the series 100, -200, -300 and -400. The latter variant now number 13, six of which are Combis, and are regularly used on Far East routes. Taxying onto runway 36L at Beijing's Capital airport is 747-426(SCD) F-GISE*

BELOW *Against the looming shape of Lion Rock, 747-426 F-GITB prepares to land at Kai Tak after a non-stop 12 hour flight from Pari*

LEFT *To commemorate France hosting the 1998 World Cup Finals, 16 aircraft were painted with a footballer along both sides of the fuselage in the team colours of all 32 finalists. The starboard side of 747-4B3 F-GEXA featured Argentina, as seen on a flight to Hong Kong in April 1998. This is one of two former U.T.A. 747-400 aircraft on the carriers inventory*

RIGHT *Air France 747-426 F-GISD gleams in the late afternoon sunshine. Is it fair to describe it as a great white whale? Not in flight*

BELOW *Air France 747-426 F-GISB gathers speed on its take-off roll on runway 13 at Kai Tak bound for Paris. Due to prevailing winds westbound flights are generally about an hour longer than those eastbound, averaging around 13 hours. The author has endured a flight from Hong Kong to Heathrow in an A340 which, with extreme headwinds and the necessity of avoiding Afghan airspace, lasted a marathon 15 hours and 10 minutes!*

BELOW *Like some other European carriers Air France has formed a subsidiary, Air France Asie to operate services to Taipei. These were operated by two 747-426(SCD) aircraft, F-GISA and SC. These aircraft have since returned to the main fleet. In addition to the Air France Asie titles the other difference in livery was the lack of a red stripe on the rudder. The series -400 no longer serves with the subsidiary, having been replaced by the Airbus A340*

U.T.A. Union de Transports Aeriens was an independent French carrier which had an extensive intercontinental network extending through Africa, the South Pacific and as far as New Zealand. The DC-10 and Boeing 747 fleet were supplemented by a pair of 747-400s which were acquired in September 1989 and July 1991, the latter being a Combi. Their career with U.T.A. was, however, short-lived, as the airline was merged into Air France on 29th December 1992. Note the BigBoss titles behind the cockpit on 747-4B3 F-GEXA (Christian Volpati)

RIGHT *El Al Israeli Airlines has operated a solely Boeing fleet for many years, and no doubt feels obligated to do so for continuing U.S. diplomatic support. The decision-making process for a new short haul aircraft involved something of an empty PR exercise, asking passengers who had only ever flown in Boeings, whether they preferred a Boeing or Airbus type! Needless to say, the Next Generation 737 was chosen. The 747 was introduced on long haul routes as long ago as May 1971, with the first of three series -400s joining the fleet in April 1994. These are operated in an F12/C42Y424 mixed configuration. With additional titles to commemorate the airline's 50th anniversary, 747-458 4X-ELB is seen on approach to London's Heathrow airport*

LEFT *Virgin Atlantic Airways is the newest European operator of the 747-400, taking delivery of its first machine on 28th April 1994, a day after El Al took delivery of its first machine. The airline's second aircraft, 747-4Q8 G-VBIG named Tinker Belle, is seen here poised to land at Gatwick after a flight from Miami*

RIGHT *Virgin Atlantic's 747-4Q8 G-VBIG Tinker Belle seen taxying past the North Terminal at its Gatwick base. Since this photograph was taken the airline has undergone a fleet rationalisation programme which has seen all six -400s based at Heathrow, while the classic Jumbos are Gatwick-based*

OPPOSITE *Because of their size 747s often have to be marshalled to their parking position at many airports around the world. Despite the stand guidance systems marshallers are still required on some parking stands at Heathrow. Here marshaller No.2 gets ready to signal stop to the No.1 marshaller who is positioned ahead of the aircraft*

BELOW RIGHT *Virgin's red and white livery stands out like a beacon in the early morning sunshine as 747-4Q8 G-VFAB Lady Penelope approaches Heathrow. Note the 'No Way BA/AA' message on the fuselage, Richard Branson's objection to the proposed merger of two of the world's largest carriers, which, in the author's opinion, certainly would not be to the passengers' benefit*

Climbing out of Gatwick bound for Miami is Virgin's Tinker Belle, 747-4Q8 G-VBIG. A few of the airline's 747-400s have personalised registrations, such as VBIG, VAST and VXLG

RIGHT *Royal Air Maroc joined the -400 club with the acquisition of 747-426 CN-RGA in October 1993. This aircraft had been built for Air France in January 1993, but immediately placed in storage at Marana until acquired by its current operator. The airline also operates a single 747-200(SCD), having disposed of the former South African Airways 747SP once operated. (Authors collection via Christian Laugier)*

BELOW RIGHT *The famous orange tail and Springbok logo has appeared on the tails of South African Airways 747 Jumbos since the type joined the fleet in October 1971. The airline still operates four variants, the series -200, -300, -400 and SP. The first of the -400s were delivered in January 1991, and the fleet now numbers six, the last being delivered on 30th November 1998. Named after the town of Kempton Park, 747-444 ZS-SAX lines up for departure from Heathrow's runway 09R bound for Johannesburg*

OVERLEAF *In 1997, South African Airways unveiled a new livery, but it is the older 747 variants which are receiving the new livery first. Still adorned in the old livery is 747-444 ZS-SAV Durban. The airline has the titling in English on the starboard side and in Afrikaans on the port*

RIGHT *Kuwait Airways added a single 747-469(SCD), 9K-ADE Al-Jabariya to its inventory in November 1994. This was to have been the first of three, but the order for the remaining two was subsequently cancelled. This particular aircraft is rarely seen for, although it operates in full Kuwait Airways livery, it is operated as a VIP aircraft on behalf of the government. It carries an official crest just behind the cockpit*

OPPOSITE, BELOW
Coincident with the delivery of new Boeing 777s and MD-90s, Saudi Arabian Airlines introduced a new livery comprising beige upper surfaces and grey undersides, with a dark blue tail, upon which are gold crossed swords and a palm tree. The scheme was introduced in time to appear on the company's first -400, 747-468 HZ-AIV. The airline has ordered five of these aircraft, all but one of which have been delivered, supplementing the extensive Jumbo Jet fleet which comprises every model, the 747-100, -200 and -300 and SP. (SPA Photography)

BELOW *Air India, a 747 operator since 1971, added the series -400 to its portfolio in August 1993. Six of the type are now in service in a 448 seat configuration split thus: F16C42Y390. That is, 16 first, 42 business and 390 economy seats. Taxying for departure at Heathrow is 747-437 VT-EVA, named after the city of Agra*

RIGHT *Late in 1989 Air India introduced a new livery which dispensed with the palace type image, but the airline was unprepared for the furore which followed. Religious leaders and the population as a whole complained so much that the decision was eventually reversed, in time for the old livery to be applied to the first of the company's 747-400s. This features palace type paintwork around the windows and 'Your Palace in the Sky' painted on the rear fuselage, as seen on 747-437 VT-EVB Velha Goa*

BELOW RIGHT *From its humble beginnings, thanks to assistance from S.A.S., Thai Airways International has become one of Asia's largest and most successful carriers. The airline is renowned for its Royal Orchid service and its imaginative livery features a stylised version of this flower on the tail. Although the airline is a strong supporter of Airbus products it also operates Boeing 747s and 777s. Wearing the name Alongkorn underneath the cockpit, 747-4D7 HS-TGK taxies to its gate at Bangkok's Don Muang airport. Thai Airways International took delivery of its first 747-200 in November 1979. All of this variant have since moved on to pastures new, the current fleet comprising a pair of series -300s and 13 -400s, with a further example of the latter to be delivered*

VT-EVB

BELOW *Captured just as the wheels clear the tarmac of runway 09R at London's Heathrow airport is Thai 747-4D7 HS-TGR Siriwatthana. Thanks to the success of tourism, load factors on the London Bangkok route are very high, and on several days of the week the airline operates two flights*

HS-TGR

Thai

RIGHT *Malaysia Airlines has acquired three variants of the Boeing 747, the series -200, -300 and -400, although only the latter is now in service. The first two -400s were taken on charge at the end of 1989, both being Combi models. Since then 11 pure passenger -400s have been added to the fleet, with a further six on order. Illustrated is 747-4H6 9M-MPD at Kai Tak with prominent 'Visit Malaysia Year '94' titles on the fuselage. The airline allocates names of Malaysian towns and cities to its 747 aircraft, with Seremban allocated to Papa Delta*

BELOW RIGHT *In recent years Malaysia Airlines has found a few reasons to add additional features to the company livery. Markings to celebrate the country's 50th anniversary appear just forward of the horizontal tailplane of 747-4H6 9M-MPE Kangar seen against the menacing looking Lion Rock while on approach to Kai Tak*

BELOW *In 1998 Malaysia Airlines took the opportunity to advertise its role as host nation for the Commonwealth Games that year. The logo for that event is seen on the rear fuselage of 9M-MHL Kuala Lumpur. This was the airline's first 747-400, and one of two 4H6(SCD) Combi variants*

RIGHT *The national airline of the tiny island nation of Singapore has a massive fleet of long-haul aircraft, including Airbus A310s and A340s, Boeing 747s and 777s. The airline is the second largest operator of the 747-400 and, when the aircraft currently on order are delivered, the fleet will number 53 aircraft, eight of which are freighters*

BELOW RIGHT *Singapore Airlines is the proud operator of the 1,000th Boeing 747 built. This aircraft, 747-412 9V-SMU, was delivered to the airline on 13th October 1993, and is seen awaiting take-off clearance from Hong Kong*

LEFT *Singapore Airlines became a 747 operator in 1977 with the first of a batch of series -200. These were followed by series -300s, dubbed Big Top in 1986. The -200s have long gone from the carrier's inventory, and only a handful of -300s now remain. The airline's series -412 passenger variant was introduced in 1989 and is dubbed the Megatop. This fleet currently numbers 37 aircraft with a further eight on order. Illustrated cranking round the corner onto final approach at Kai Tak is 747-412 9V-SMO*

To celebrate the country's 50th year as an independent state in 1997, Singapore Airlines Boeing 747-412 9V-SMZ received additional golden ribbon markings along the fuselage

RIGHT *In September 1998 Singapore Airlines unveiled plans for a completely revamped interior for its Boeing 747-400 fleet, with the emphasis on its first class product. To promote this, two aircraft (9V-SPK & SPL) were painted in a Tropical Megatop scheme, with 9V-SPL making its first flight in this livery to London Heathrow (SPA Photography)*

BELOW LEFT *1998 was not a good year for Garuda Indonesia Airways. The troubles started in January when the airline was unable to complete payment on a number of new Boeing 737s, which resulted in them being flown to the southern U.S. for desert storage. Further damage was inevitable with the Asian economic crisis, in which the Rupiah was drastically devalued, closely followed by severe political unrest, which had a major effect on tourism. Many seats on the airline's network were left unsold, including those on the Boeing 747s, like PK-GSI, the former Varig 747-441 illustrated*

Following this catalogue of woes Garuda acted to cut costs, the first measure being the disposal of the six strong MD-11 fleet. Services to Europe were cut back to just three cities, Amsterdam, Frankfurt and London. Since the disposal of the MD-11s, the fleet of three Boeing 747-400s have taken over the thrice-weekly service to London/Gatwick. This is 747-4U3 PK-GSG at the point of rotation at the London airport. Garuda's 747 fleet comprises six series -200s and three -400s. One of the latter model is a former Varig aircraft acquired on lease from ILFC in March 1995, joining two newly built 747-4U3 aircraft which were delivered a year earlier. The first of that pair is PK-GSG

RIGHT *Philippine Airlines is an Asian carrier which has suffered even more than Garuda. A combination of economic trouble combined with a series of damaging strikes forced the airline to cease operations on 23rd September 1998. A few weeks later, limited international services were restarted, though the airline had to go to the courts to acquire the three 747-400s which had been impounded by creditors. Orders for further examples have now been cancelled, and one aircraft, which had been fully painted and was awaiting delivery in June 1998, has been acquired by Air New Zealand. Philippines' 747-4F6 N752PR is seen at Hong Kong in happier times*

BELOW LEFT *Philippine Airlines has operated a total of four 747-400s, including one Combi. The first example was 747-4F6 N751PR acquired on lease in November 1993, seen on final approach to Kai Tak in April 1998*

Taiwan's China Airlines has been a 747 operator since June 1976 when it leased a series -100 from Delta Airlines. The following year the airline took delivery of its first 747SP, with the series -200 joining the fleet in 1978. Both the SP and -200 are still in service, alongside a fleet of series -400s which steadily grows. Boeing 747-409 B-163 was the third of an initial batch of five ordered, and is seen inbound to Kai Tak

RIGHT *China Airlines is the only operator that has lost a 747-400 in an accident. To cover fro the loss of 747-409 B-165 off the end of the runway at Kai Tak on 4th November 1993, Singapore Airlines' 747-412 9V-SMC was leased to China Airlines for three years from 1st June 1994. In the Taiwanese carrier's service the aircraft operated under the registration 3B-SMC, and is seen on its take-off roll on runway 13 at Kai Tak for the short flight to Taipei*

BELOW *The short 75-minute flight between Hong Kong and Taipei is operated by a number of Asian carriers, though needless to say, China Airlines and Cathay Pacific supply the majority of flights. On this heavily travelled route China Airlines operates a number of types, from the A300 to the MD-11 and Boeing 747. Boeing 747-200s are often used, but more frequent use of the larger -400 is now being made. On this occasion it is 747-412 3B-SMC, the leased Singapore Airlines example*

OPPOSITE, BELOW *In 1996 China Airlines unveiled a progressive new livery which, for the first time, dispensed with the national flag, making it easier to operate to countries that do not wish to upset the authorities in Beijing. The new livery features a large hibiscus, as on the tail of this 747-409 preparing to depart Los Angeles*

China Airlines 747-400 fleet has now risen to 11, with one more on order. Four of the type joined the fleet in 1997, including B-18203 seen here climbing out of Anchorage

RIGHT *Mandarin Airlines, a subsidiary of China Airlines, was formed in 1991, and now operates all the parent company's MD-11 tri-jets. A single 747-409 joined the fleet directly on its delivery from Boeing in June 1995, and this aircraft is used primarily on the Taipei Vancouver route on behalf of the parent company. The aircraft concerned, B-16801 is illustrated poised for landing at the Canadian gateway in June 1998. It is likely that this aircraft will join the fleet of China Airlines, as this parent company has decided to merge Mandarin with Formosa Airlines, retain the former name, but operate domestic services only*

OPPOSITE, BELOW *A member of the Evergreen Group of companies, Eva Air was formed in 1989, and has steadily built up its fleet to over 30 aircraft, all but three of which are wide-bodies. The Boeing 747 and MD-11 predominate, most of the latter being the freighter variant. The airline took delivery of its first Jumbo, 747-45E B-16401 in November 1992, which was photographed soon afterwards at London/Gatwick, having replaced the Boeing 767s previously used on this service*

BELOW *The Eva Air 747-400 fleet is now larger than national carrier China Airlines, and now numbers 15 aircraft, 10 of which are the Combi model. One of the Combis is 747-45E(SCD) B-16463, seen inbound to Kai Tak in May 1998. Note the huge size of the flaps*

RIGHT *Six of Eva's 747 fleet are leased aircraft and operate under U.S. registrations, including 747-45E(SCD) N406EV seen taxying clear of the runway at Kai Tak. Sister ships N403EV and 405EV were built as passenger aircraft but have been converted to SCD Combi standard*

OPPOSITE *As Hong Kong features heavily in this book, not unnaturally, so does Cathay Pacific. Due to the economic situation in Asia the airline is disposing of its 747-200s, and it has announced the series -300s will be sold or withdrawn by October 1999. The 747-400 fleet currently stands at 19 passenger aircraft and two freighters*

BELOW *With a background of towering apartment blocks and imposing mountain it could only be Kai Tak. Cathay's 747-467 VR-HUE thunders down runway 13 on its take-off roll. The take-off run of a heavily laden 747-400 bound for Western Europe lasts almost a full minute*

Early morning arrival meets early morning departure at Kai Tak, surely one of the most dramatic and photogenic airports in the world

RIGHT *Cathay's VR-HOO taxies to ramp after landing on runway 13 at Kai Tak. In the background the buildings on Hong Kong Island are clearly visible, while the strip of water in the foreground is the rather noxious nullah*

BELOW *As well as marathon trips to Western Europe or Los Angeles, Catha's 747-400s are also used to supplement smaller types on high-density regional routes such as Taipei or Manila. VR-HOZ has been in service with the airline since June 1992*

BELOW *Boeing 747-467 VR-HOU departs Gatwick for the 12-hour non-stop flight to Hong Kong. Cathay has since moved its London operation to Heathrow, seemingly under the mistaken impression that passengers prefer this overcrowded location. Note the Union Jack on the fin of the aircraft. These were removed from the airline's fleet several years prior to the 1997 hand-over of Hong Kong to China*

Following the hand-over to China, Hong Kong-based aircraft have changed their VR-Hxx. registrations to B-Hxx. Wearing its Chinese registration is 747-467 B-HUB

RIGHT *Cathay Pacific's new for 1994 livery. The grand surprise was spoiled by the delivery of liveried vehicles before the event. 747-467 VR-HO was the first to receive the new scheme*

BELOW *Victoria Harbour passes to starboard as Cathay 747-467 B-HOV lifts off runway 13 bound for Tokyo*

BELOW *Air China has in recent years expanded its 747 fleet with significant numbers of -400 series aircraft,, so much so that this model now outnumbers earlier SP and -200 variants. The airline currently operates five pure passenger 747-4J6 aircraft, including B-2443. One more was on order for 1999 delivery*

B-2460 is captured in dramatic fashion midway through the 47° right turn to align with runway 13 at Kai Tak, seemingly surrounded by apartment blocks. Air China has seven Combi 400s on strength with a further example on order

RIGHT *With everything hanging, an Air China 747-4J6(SCD) inbound to runway 13 is about to make the same turn*

BELOW *Air China 747-4J6(SCD) at the holding point for runway 36L at Beijing's Capital airport. The airline is in the process of taking delivery of Airbus A340s and Boeing 777s to augment its long haul fleet*

LEFT *Korean Air is fast attaining a reputation as the world's most accident-prone airline, and in 1998 it suffered five accidents or incidents in as many months. One of these involved 747-400 HL7496 which, whilst landing on runway 14r at Seoul's Kimpo airport overran the runway, ripping off the undercarriage in the process. The aircraft is, however, likely to be repaired. The airline's large Jumbo jet fleet includes 28 series -400s, one of which is a Combi and three are freighters. This is 747-4B5 HL7489*

RIGHT *Korean Air's 747-400s are used primarily to U.S. destinations and to Western Europe, though the Asian economic downturn has seen the carrier utilise smaller types like the 747SP and 777 on some European routes, as passenger numbers have dropped off dramatically. The situation has become so bad that many of the foreign carriers have ceased service to Seoul, though that at least should help the Korean national carrier. Illustrated climbing out of Los Angeles is 747-4B5 HL7478. When deliveries of the four series -400s on order are complete, the airline will have 29 of the type, one of which is a Combi*

BELOW *Asiana's growing fleet of 747-400s currently includes three each of the passenger, Combi and freighter variants, with five, two and one respectively on order. The economic downturn means that it is likely that some or all of those on order will never be delivered and new customers found as the airline strives to cut costs. One -400 in service has already been sold to Qantas, whilst one of those on order has been placed in storage at Marana. Awaiting take-off clearance from Kai Tak is Asiana 747-48E HL7417*

LEFT *Asiana Airlines was formed in 1988, and initial operations were undertaken by Boeing 737-400s. Early operations were severely restricted by the South Korean Government in order to protect Korean Air, though these were gradually lifted, and the airline now operates intercontinental routes. The 737s are still used on domestic and regional services, now supported by new A321s. Long haul and high-density regional routes are operated by Boeing 767s and 747s, while 777s and A330s are on order. Wearing titles to promote Korean tourism in 1994 is 747-48E(SCD) HL7415*

RIGHT *Boeing developed the -400(D) high-density variant for All Nippon and Japan Airlines domestic routes. All Nippon has taken delivery of 11 of this model, which operate in a 569-seat configuration with 27 business and 542 economy seats. Because of the short sectors involved, these aircraft are not fitted with winglets, and can be identified by the additional windows in the upper deck. On the 400(D) there are 20 windows, as opposed to 15 in the standard long range 400. Taxying for departure at Osaka's Itami domestic airport bound for Tokyo/Haneda is All Nippon 747-481(D) JA8963*

OPPOSITE, BELOW
*Were you paying attention
to the caption opposite?
Then you may be confused
by this shot of All Nippon
747-481 JA8955 about to
land at Osaka/Kansai
airport. True, the aircraft
has the 20 upper deck
windows fitted to the
400(D), yet has winglets.
The reason is that this is
one of two All Nippon
747-481(D) aircraft which
have been converted to
long range standard*

LEFT *Japan Airlines
operates its eight-strong
747-446(D) fleet in a
568 seat configuration;
C24Y544, varying very
slightly from that of All
Nippon. The airline
competes with its rival on
several domestic routes,
including the one-hour-long
Tokyo -Osaka run. Featured
at the latter location is
JA8083*

RIGHT *Japan Airlines'
747-446(D) JA8904
poised for touchdown
at Osaka/Itami airport.
The airline has allocated
the name Sky Cruiser to
its 747-400s, though the
words have not yet been
painted on every aircraft.*

BELOW RIGHT *Japan
Airlines' 747-446 JA8910
leaves behind a crowded
ramp on its take-off run
at Kai Tak.*

OPPOSITE *Delivered in
January 1990, JA8071
was the first 747-446
for Japan Airlines*

Climbing into the late afternoon skies over Kansai is Japan Airlines' 747-446 JA8902. In addition to the eight 446(D) models, the airline has 30 long range 747-446s on its inventory, with a further 14 to be delivered

RIGHT *The white fuselage of 747-446 JA8910 almost glows against the moody skies and menacing mountains in the background. Japan Airlines has been a 747 operator since April 1970, and it still operates a few ageing series -100s. In November 1998 the airline took delivery of its 100th 747 from Boeing, and although a number of earlier aircraft have been disposed of, the airline's Jumbo fleet count currently stands at an amazing 85 aircraft*

BELOW *For Presidential and VIP use the Japanese Government took delivery of a pair of 747-47C aircraft in the autumn of 1991. These were originally registered JA8091 and 8092, however on 1st April 1992 they were transferred to the Japanese Air Self-Defence Force (JASDF) who operate them on behalf of the government with the military registration 20-1101 and 02*

LEFT *Even at low level, the wing flex on the 747-400 is quite noticeable. Only seconds from touchdown on Kai Tak's runway 13, JAL's 747-446 JA8911 is still in a banking turn. Until the Asian economic downturn the Tokyo-Hong Kong route was one of the most lucrative in the world*

Qantas, the Australian national carrier, has operated 747 Jumbos since it took delivery of the first of 22 series -200s on the last day of July 1971. A handful of these remain, alongside the two 747SPs and six series -300s delivered since. The first of 18 series -400s on order arrived in August 1989, with deliveries completed by October 1992. In clean configuration soon after take-off from Manchester's Ringway airport is 747-438 VH-OJG City of Hobart. Qantas aircraft are unmistakable thanks to the all-white fuselage and bright red fin with its kangaroo. Promoting the aircraft's range, the airline has dubbed the type Longreach. A further three aircraft are on order for delivery from late 1999, while one Asiana and two former Malaysia Airlines aircraft have recently been incorporated into the fleet

RIGHT & BELOW *Originally named* City of Sydney, *Qantas 747-438 VH-OJB was adorned in this amazing paint scheme in time to perform a flypast at the 1994 SBAC Farnborough Air Show. Entitled* Wunala Dreaming, *the scheme was devised to celebrate Australia's Aboriginal cultural heritage. A similar theme in turquoise,* Nalanji Dreaming, *adorns one of the company's 747-300s, and both schemes have been chosen as part of the British Airways Utopia world images. They adorn the tails of a few of that carrier's aircraft. The vibrant scheme is shown off at Heathrow, showing both the starboard and port sides*

LEFT *The centre fuselage is enshrouded in a cloud of moisture as Qantas 747-438 VH-OJQ* City of Mandurah *appears through the murk inbound to Kai Tak in March 1998*

RIGHT *In recent years the 747-400 fleet of Air New Zealand has been increased to seven aircraft with the acquisition of two former Varig aircraft on lease from I.L.F.C. In October 1998 it also added an aircraft originally destined for Philippine Airlines, when that carrier hit financial problems. Former Varig 747-441 is illustrated in Air New Zealand marks as ZK-SUI*

BELOW RIGHT *Air New Zealand has been operating 747s since May 1981 when it acquired its first series -200s. The first -400 was delivered in December 1989, five months behind schedule. Soon afterwards, the type was utilised on the service to London/Gatwick. Several years earlier the carrier had suspended DC-10 services to London/Heathrow. Taxying from Gatwick's North Terminal for the one-stop flight to Auckland is 747-419 ZK-NBT*

LEFT *In 1996 Air New Zealand unveiled a new livery which dispensed with the blue and turquoise cheatline. The tail logo of the Maori symbol Koru is retained, but on a graduated blue background. The scheme is shown to good effect on 747-419 ZK-NBS on its approach to runway 27R at Heathrow in December 1997*

BELOW LEFT *Air New Zealand has moved its London gateway from Gatwick to Heathrow, and has now increased the frequency to a daily service. The carrier has recently completely revamped its cabins, and even in economy class, seats are fitted with legrest and head supports. Added to the already excellent in-flight service, this puts the carrier streets ahead of its competitor on the route, United Airlines. Having experienced the service of both carriers on the London Los Angeles Auckland route, for the author there is only one choice*

Chapter Two

BOEING 747-400F FREIGHTER

BELOW *The latest 747-400F operator is Atlas Air Cargo, the only U.S. operator of the type. This Carrier specialises in operating cargo schedules on behalf of major carriers, and customers include airlines such as British Airways, S.A.S. and Swissair. Atlas received its first -400F on 29th July 1998, and currently operates three, with a further six due. Photographed on a rain-soaked runway at Prestwick whilst operating for Cargolux is 747-47UF N492MC. This aircraft carries the name* Spirit of Panalpina *on the nose, in honour of the well known freight forwarder*

Following the success of freighter variants of earlier model 747s, it was inevitable that such a variant of the -400 would follow. The 400F has the same fuselage as the -200F, with the short upper deck. It also has the upward opening nose cone, as well as the side cargo door in the port rear fuselage, with the standard cargo doors in the lower belly as in passenger models.

The strengthened cabin floor includes an improved cargo handling system, and despite the stronger and larger wing, the -400F is actually slightly lighter than the -200F. Total cargo volume is 27,467 cu.ft (777.8m^3), of which 21,347 cu.ft (604.5m^3) is on the main deck. The main deck can accommodate 30 standard cargo pallets with 32 LD-1 containers and bulk loads in the belly hold. The aircraft is capable of carrying a 249,000 lb (113,000 kg) load a distance of 4,400nm (8,100 km), and freight operator Cargolux estimates this capability will allow the airline to dispense with some 300 fuelling stops a year. At first, it was thought that the type would dispense with the winglets, and although the author has seen the aircraft operate in this manner, this did not prove to be the case, and winglets are standard.

The first -400F (N6005C) flew on 4th May 1993 and the type entered service with Cargolux in November that year. Although the Luxembourg-based carrier was the first recipient, it was Air France which was first to order the type, but this order was subsequently cancelled. There are presently six operators of the 747-400F, four of which are in Asia ; Asiana, Cathay Pacific, Korean Air and Singapore Airlines. In view of its large 747 freighter fleet it is perhaps surprising that Japan Airlines has not joined this club. The remaining operators are Cargolux and the U.S. freight carrier Atlas Air.

One future recipient of the type will be the U.S.A.F., which has eight -400F airframes on order intended to be used as the platform for a laser based anti-missile defence system. These have been given the rather clumsy and unmemorable designation AL-1A.

TOP *Having at one time said that it saw no need to acquire the 400F, Cargolux will soon be the largest operator of the type. The airline currently has five in service, and the order early in December 1998 for a further two takes the outstanding orders to six aircraft. The carrier's first of the type entered service in November 1993, and they are used on ultra-long-range sectors where the aircraft's range has allowed Cargolux to dispense with some of the refuelling stops required by the 747-200F. Illustrated on the taxiway at Taipei's Chiang Kai Shek International Airport is 747-428F LX-ICV City of Ettelbruck, Grand Duchy of Luxembourg. This aircraft was destined for, but then cancelled by, Air France*

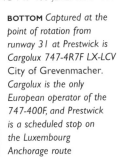

BOTTOM *Captured at the point of rotation from runway 31 at Prestwick is Cargolux 747-4R7F LX-LCV City of Grevenmacher. Cargolux is the only European operator of the 747-400F, and Prestwick is a scheduled stop on the Luxembourg Anchorage route*

Despite having a modest fleet of 747-400s, Asiana Airlines was quick to realise the -400F was the ideal aircraft to inaugurate its new long haul cargo schedules. The airline now has three of these freighters in service, with another to follow. Flights from Seoul to the U.S. route via Anchorage. Caught against a spectacular background as it rotates from runway 32 at the Alaskan gateway is 747-48EF HL7419

OPPOSITE, TOP *Like rival Asiana, Korean Air has adopted the -400F to boost its substantial fleet of 747 freighters. The airline has ordered four to date, three of which are already in service. The fourth has been built, but placed in storage and a buyer sought. These aircraft are heavily utilised on services to the U.S., for which Anchorage is a strategic gateway. Korean Air 747-4B5F HL7497 is seen climbing into the crystal clear Alaskan skies on departure from Anchorage*

OPPOSITE, BOTTOM
It really was no surprise when Cathay Pacific chose the 747-400F, as the airline had already selected and was operating the -400 passenger model. It also had a few series -200 freighters. Cathay has taken delivery of two -400Fs, in May 1994 and July 1995. The first was therefore delivered in the airline's old livery while the second is in the new one. The airline uses these aircraft on services both to Europe and the U.S., the latter route through Anchorage, where 747-467F B-HUH is photographed soon after departure

LEFT *Singapore Airlines' 747-400F, the Mega Ark. It has even put the name and company logo on the underside of the nose, so that when it is open they are visible*

RIGHT *Singapore Airlines' 747-400 aircraft are powered by Pratt & Whitney PW4056 engines. The rear of the cowling gleams on this newly delivered 400F*

BELOW *Like the other Asian operators of the 747-400F, Anchorage is a regular stopping-off point for Singapore Airlines 747-412F fleet. Mega Ark 9V-SFB is seen departing the Alaskan airport. The airline has just one aircraft left to fulfil its order for eight of these freighters*

A close look at the winglet on a Mega Ark during a turn round at Sharjah

MAIN IMAGE *Under northern skies, with the Alaska Range in the background, Singapore's first 747-412F Mega Ark, 9V-SFA enters runway 14 at Anchorage*

INSET *Singapore Airlines' freighter fleet operates westwards to Europe and eastwards to the U.S. The airline also operates freighter services on behalf of Lufthansa, and it is not uncommon to see three or four Mega Arks in a day at Sharjah, the German carrier's Middle East freight hub. Note the auxiliary power unit (APU) exhausts protruding from the extreme rear fuselage*

Boeing 747-400

1 Radome
2 Weather radar scanner
3 Front pressure bulkhead
4 Scanner tracking mechanism
5 Wardrobe
6 First-class cabin, 30 or 34 seats at 62-in [1.57-m] pitch
7 Nose undercarriage wheel bay
8 Nosewheel doors
9 Twin nosewheels
10 Hydraulic steering jacks
11 Nose undercarriage pivot mounting
12 Underfloor avionics equipment racks
13 Cabin window panels
14 First-class bar unit
15 Flight deck floor level
16 Rudder pedals
17 Control yoke
18 Instrument panel, five-CRT EFIS displays
19 Instrument panel shroud
20 Windscreen panels
21 Overhead systems switch panel
22 First Officer's seat
23 Captain's seat [two-crew cockpit]
24 Observer's folding seats [2]
25 Starboard side toilet compartments [2]
26 Cockpit bulkhead
27 Crew rest bunks [2]
28 Upper deck window panel
29 Conditioned-air distribution ducting
30 Forward main deck galley unit
31 Plug-type forward cabin door, No 1 port and starboard
32 Business-class passenger seating, 24 seats typical at 36-in [91-cm] pitch
33 Fuselage lower lobe skin panelling
34 Baggage/cargo pallet containers
35 Forward under-floor cargo hold, capacity 2,768 cu ft [78.4 cu m]
36 Forward fuselage frame and stringer construction
37 Upper deck doorway, port and starboard
38 Cabin roof frames
39 Anti-collision beacon light
40 No.1 UHF communications antenna
41 Upper deck passenger cabin, 52 business-class or 69 economy-class seats
42 Lower deck sidewall toilet compartment
43 No 2 passenger door, port and starboard
44 Air conditioning system heat exchanger intake ducting
45 Ventral ram air intakes
46 Faired wing root leading edge fillet
47 Ventral air conditioning packs, port and starboard
48 Wing spar bulkhead

49 Economy-class seating
50 Staircase to upper deck level
51 Fresh-water tanks
52 Wing centre-section fuel tankage, capacity 16,990 US gal [64,315 litres]
53 Centre-section stringer construction
54 Floor beam structure

55 Front spar/ fuselage main frame
56 Upper deck lobby area
57 Curtained bulkhead
58 Galley units
59 Starboard wing inboard main fuel tank, capacity 12,546 US gal [47,492 litres]
60 Fuel pumps
61 Engine bleed air supply ducting
62 Krueger flap operating mechanism
63 Inboard Krueger flap segments
64 Inboard Pratt & Whitney PW4256 engine nacelle
65 Inboard nacelle pylon
66 Leading-edge Krueger flap segments
67 Pressure refuelling connections, port and starboard
68 Krueger flap drive shaft
69 Krueger flap rotary actuators
70 Starboard wing outer main fuel tank, capacity 4,482 US gal [16,966 litres]
71 Starboard outer engine nacelle
72 Outer nacelle pylon
73 Starboard wing reserve tank provision, capacity 534 US gal 2,021 litres]
74 Outboard Krueger flap
75 Krueger flap drive mechanism
76 Outer wing panel dry bay
77 Vent surge tank

78 Wing-tip extension
79 Starboard navigation [green] and strobe [white] lights
80 Starboard winglet
81 Fixed portion of trailing edge
82 Fuel vent
83 Static dischargers
84 Outboard, low-speed, aileron
85 Outboard four-segment spoilers
86 Outboard triple-slotted Fowler-type flap, extended
87 Flap screw jacks and segment linkages
88 Flap drive shaft
89 Inboard, high speed, aileron
90 Inboard triple-slotted flap, extended
91 Inboard two-segment spoilers/lift dumpers
92 Inboard triple-slotted flap, extended
93 Auxiliary trailing edge wing spar
94 Cabin air distribution ducting
95 Extended upper deck rear bulkhead
96 Upper deck floor beams
97 Air system cross-feed ducting
98 Conditioned-air risers
99 Machined wing spar attaching main frames
100 Central flap drive motors
101 Wing-mounted outboard main undercarriage wheel bay
102 Undercarriage mounting beam
103 Central keel section
104 Pressure floor above wheel bay
105 Centre fuselage frame and stringer construction

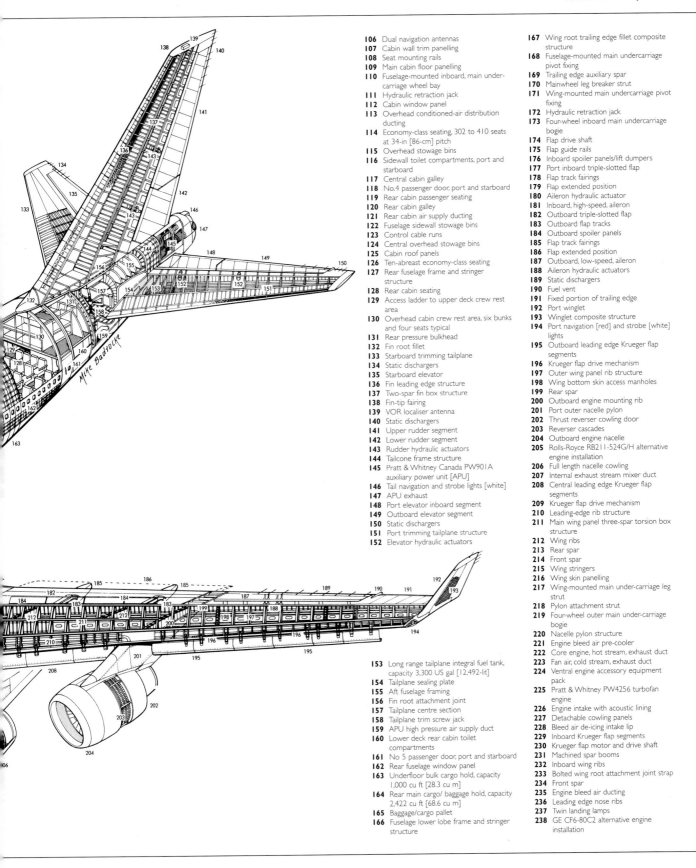

106 Dual navigation antennas
107 Cabin wall trim panelling
108 Seat mounting rails
109 Main cabin floor panelling
110 Fuselage-mounted inboard, main under-carriage wheel bay
111 Hydraulic retraction jack
112 Cabin window panel
113 Overhead conditioned-air distribution ducting
114 Economy-class seating, 302 to 410 seats at 34-in [86-cm] pitch
115 Overhead stowage bins
116 Sidewall toilet compartments, port and starboard
117 Central cabin galley
118 No.4 passenger door, port and starboard
119 Rear cabin passenger seating
120 Rear cabin galley
121 Rear cabin air supply ducting
122 Fuselage sidewall stowage bins
123 Control cable runs
124 Central overhead stowage bins
125 Cabin roof panels
126 Ten-abreast economy-class seating
127 Rear fuselage frame and stringer structure
128 Rear cabin seating
129 Access ladder to upper deck crew rest area
130 Overhead cabin crew rest area, six bunks and four seats typical
131 Rear pressure bulkhead
132 Fin root fillet
133 Starboard trimming tailplane
134 Static dischargers
135 Starboard elevator
136 Fin leading edge structure
137 Two-spar fin box structure
138 Fin-tip fairing
139 VOR localiser antenna
140 Static dischargers
141 Upper rudder segment
142 Lower rudder segment
143 Rudder hydraulic actuators
144 Tailcone frame structure
145 Pratt & Whitney Canada PW901A auxiliary power unit [APU]
146 Tail navigation and strobe lights [white]
147 APU exhaust
148 Port elevator inboard segment
149 Outboard elevator segment
150 Static dischargers
151 Port trimming tailplane structure
152 Elevator hydraulic actuators

153 Long range tailplane integral fuel tank, capacity 3,300 US gal [12,492-lit]
154 Tailplane sealing plate
155 Aft fuselage framing
156 Fin root attachment joint
157 Tailplane centre section
158 Tailplane trim screw jack
159 APU high pressure air supply duct
160 Lower deck rear cabin toilet compartments
161 No 5 passenger door, port and starboard
162 Rear fuselage window panel
163 Underfloor bulk cargo hold, capacity 1,000 cu ft [28.3 cu m]
164 Rear main cargo/ baggage hold, capacity 2,422 cu ft [68.6 cu m]
165 Baggage/cargo pallet
166 Fuselage lower lobe frame and stringer structure

167 Wing root trailing edge fillet composite structure
168 Fuselage-mounted main undercarriage pivot fixing
169 Trailing edge auxiliary spar
170 Mainwheel leg breaker strut
171 Wing-mounted main undercarriage pivot fixing
172 Hydraulic retraction jack
173 Four-wheel inboard main undercarriage bogie
174 Flap drive shaft
175 Flap guide rails
176 Inboard spoiler panels/lift dumpers
177 Port inboard triple-slotted flap
178 Flap track fairings
179 Flap extended position
180 Aileron hydraulic actuator
181 Inboard, high-speed, aileron
182 Outboard triple-slotted flap
183 Outboard flap tracks
184 Outboard spoiler panels
185 Flap track fairings
186 Flap extended position
187 Outboard, low-speed, aileron
188 Aileron hydraulic actuators
189 Static dischargers
190 Fuel vent
191 Fixed portion of trailing edge
192 Port winglet
193 Winglet composite structure
194 Port navigation [red] and strobe [white] lights
195 Outboard leading edge Krueger flap segments
196 Krueger flap drive mechanism
197 Outer wing panel rib structure
198 Wing bottom skin access manholes
199 Rear spar
200 Outboard engine mounting rib
201 Port outer nacelle pylon
202 Thrust reverser cowling door
203 Reverser cascades
204 Outboard engine nacelle
205 Rolls-Royce RB211-524G/H alternative engine installation
206 Full length nacelle cowling
207 Internal exhaust stream mixer duct
208 Central leading edge Krueger flap segments
209 Krueger flap drive mechanism
210 Leading-edge rib structure
211 Main wing panel three-spar torsion box structure
212 Wing ribs
213 Rear spar
214 Front spar
215 Wing stringers
216 Wing skin panelling
217 Wing-mounted main under-carriage leg strut
218 Pylon attachment strut
219 Four-wheel outer main under-carriage bogie
220 Nacelle pylon structure
221 Engine bleed air pre-cooler
222 Core engine, hot stream, exhaust duct
223 Fan air, cold stream, exhaust duct
224 Ventral engine accessory equipment pack
225 Pratt & Whitney PW4256 turbofan engine
226 Engine intake with acoustic lining
227 Detachable cowling panels
228 Bleed air de-icing intake lip
229 Inboard Krueger flap segments
230 Krueger flap motor and drive shaft
231 Machined spar booms
232 Inboard wing ribs
233 Bolted wing root attachment joint strap
234 Front spar
235 Engine bleed air ducting
236 Leading edge nose ribs
237 Twin landing lamps
238 GE CF6-80C2 alternative engine installation

Appendices

BOEING 747-400 PRODUCTION AND CUSTOMERS				
CUSTOMER	-400	-400(D)	-400(M)	-400(F)
AIR CANADA	–	–	3	–
AIR CHINA	5+1	–	7+1	–
AIR FRANCE	7	–	6	–
(Air France Asie)	–	–	*	–
AIR INDIA	6	–	–	–
AIR NEW ZEALAND	7+1	–	–	–
ALL NIPPON AWYS	11+2	9	–	–
ASIANA	3+5	–	3+2	3+1
ATLAS AIR CARGO	–	–	–	3+6
BRITISH AWYS	48+7	–	–	–
BRITISH ASIA AWYS	2	–	–	–
CANADIAN A/L INTL	4	–	–	–
CARGOLUX	–	–	–	5+6
CATHAY PACIFIC AWYS	19	–	–	2
CHINA A/L	11+1	–	–	–
(Condor)	–	–	*	–
EL AL	3+1	–	–	–
EVA AIR	5	–	10	–
GARUDA INDONESIA	3	–	–	–
JAPAN A/L	28+14	8	–	–
JAPANESE A.F. / GOVT	2	–	–	–

CUSTOMER	-400	-400(D)	-400(M)	-400(F)
K.L.M.	5	–	10+1	–
K.L.M. ASIA	–	–	4	–
KOREAN AIR	24+4	–	1	3+1
KUWAIT AWYS (op for Govt)	–	–	1	–
LUFTHANSA	15+7	–	7	–
MALAYSIA A/L	13+6	–	2	–
MANDARIN A/L	1	–	–	–
NORTHWEST A/L	10+4	–	–	–
PHILIPPINE A/L	3	–	1	–
QANTAS	21+3	–	–	–
ROYAL AIR MAROC	1	–	–	–
SAUDI ARABIAN A/L	4+1	–	–	–
SINGAPORE A/L	37+8	–	–	7+1
SOUTH AFRICAN AWYS	6	–	–	–
SULTAN of BRUNEI	1	–	–	–
THAI AWYS INTL	13+1	–	–	–
UNITED A/L	35+16	–	–	–
U.S.A.F. (YAL-1A)	–	–	–	0+8
(U.T.A.)	*	–	*	–
VARIG	*+6	–	–	–
VIRGIN ATLANTIC AWYS	6+1	–	–	–

(Correct to 30 November 1998)

SPECIFICATIONS AND COMPARISONS		
	B747-100	**B747-400**
First flight date	9 February 1969	29 April 1988
Max. accommodation	516	569
Wing span	195 ft 8 in (59.64 m)	213 ft 0 in (64.92 m) fully fuelled
Length	231 ft 10 in (70.66 m)	231 ft 10 in (70.66 m)
Height	63 ft 5 in (19.33 m)	63 ft 5 in (19.33 m)
Max. take-off weight	750,000 lb (340,195 kg)	875,000 lb (396,895 kg)
Max. range	5,527 miles (8,895 km)	8,320 miles (15,410 km)
Max. cruising speed	604 mph (973 km/h)	612 mph (985 km/h)
Service ceiling	45,000 ft (13,715 m)	45,000 ft (13,715 m)

MODEL	No. ORDERED	No. DELIVERED
B747-400	442	356
B747-400D	19	19
B747-400M	59	56
B747-400F	46	22
Total ;	566	453

(As at 30 November 1998)

* Top panel, no longer in service

+ Top panel, on order